The Night Before Christmas

ILLUSTRATED BY GILL GUILE

Brimax Books · Newmarket · England

'Twas the night before Christmas,
When all through the house
Not a creature was stirring,
Not even a mouse;
The stockings were hung
By the chimney with care,
In hopes that St Nicholas
Soon would be there;
The children were nestled
All snug in their beds,
While visions of sugar plums
Danced in their heads.

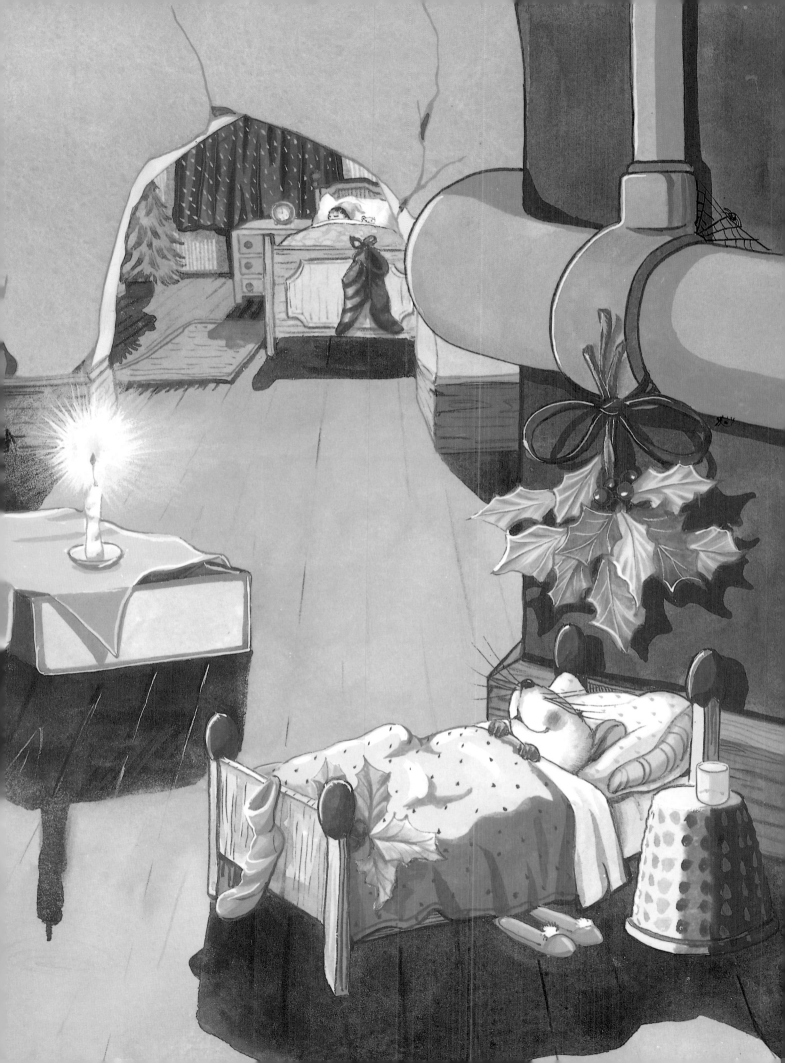

And Mamma in her 'kerchief,
And I in my cap,
Had just settled our brains
For a long winter's nap,
When out on the lawn
There arose such a clatter,
I sprang from the bed
To see what was the matter.
Away to the window
I flew like a flash,
Tore open the shutters
And threw up the sash.

The moon, on the breast
Of the new fallen snow,
Gave the lustre of mid-day
To objects below,
When what to my wondering
Eyes should appear,
But a miniature sleigh,
And eight tiny reindeer,
With a little old driver,
So lively and quick,
I knew in a moment
It must be St Nick.

More rapid than eagles
His coursers they came,
And he whistled and shouted,
And called them by name;
"Now, Dasher! Now, Dancer!
Now, Prancer and Vixen!
On, Comet! On, Cupid!
On, Donner and Blitzen
To the top of the porch!
To the top of the wall!
Now, dash away! Dash away!
Dash away all!"

As dry leaves that before
The wild hurricane fly,
When they meet with an obstacle,
Mount to the sky;
So up to the housetop
The coursers they flew,
With the sleigh full of toys,
And St Nicholas too.

And then, in a twinkling,
I heard on the roof
The prancing and pawing
Of each little hoof –
As I drew in my head,
And was turning around,
Down the chimney St Nicholas
Came with a bound.

He was dressed all in fur,
From his head to his foot,
And his clothes were all tarnished
With ashes and soot;
A bundle of toys he had
Flung on his back,
And he looked like a pedlar
Just opening his pack.
His eyes – how they twinkled!
His dimples, how merry!
His cheeks were like roses,
His nose like a cherry.

His droll little mouth
Was drawn up like a bow,
And the beard of his chin
Was as white as the snow;
The stump of his pipe he held
Tight in his teeth,
And the smoke it encircled
His head like a wreath;
He had a broad face
And a little round belly
That shook, when he laughed,
Like a bowlful of jelly.

He was chubby and plump,
A right jolly old elf,
And I laughed, when I saw him,
In spite of myself;
A wink of his eye
And a twist of his head,
Soon gave me to know
I had nothing to dread;
He spoke not a word,
But went straight to his work,
And filled all the stockings;
Then turned with a jerk,

And laying his finger
Aside of his nose,
And giving a nod,
Up the chimney he rose;
He sprang to his sleigh,
To his team gave a whistle,
And away they all flew
Like the down of a thistle.
But I heard him exclaim,
Ere he drove out of sight,
"Happy Christmas to all,
And to all a good night."

Clement C Moore

Jingle bells! Jingle bells!
Jingle all the way,
Oh, what fun it is to ride
In a one-horse open sleigh.

Dashing through the snow,
In a one-horse open sleigh,
Merrily we go,
Laughing all the way.

Bells on bob-sleigh ring,
Making spirits bright,
Oh, what fun it is to ride
In a one-horse sleigh tonight.

Jingle bells! Jingle bells!
Jingle all the way,
Oh, what fun it is to ride
In a one-horse open sleigh.

Say these words again.

moon	snow
chimney	plump
window	reindeer
whistled	house
sleigh	soot
roof	teeth
bundle	twinkled